Three Dragon Day

David Tait

smith|doorstop

Published 2015 by
smith|doorstop Books
The Poetry Business
Bank Street Arts
32–40 Bank Street
Sheffield S1 2DS

Copyright © David Tait 2015
All Rights Reserved

ISBN 978-1-910367-49-0
Typeset by Utter
Printed by People for Print, Sheffield

Acknowledgements
Many thanks to the editors of the following for publishing
these poems: *Ambit*, *Magma*, *The North*, *Poetry News* and
The Rialto

I'd also like to thank The Society of Authors for granting an
Eric Gregory Award in 2014.

Many of these poems focus on air pollution in China
To learn more about the extent of the issue, I'd like to
recommend the documentary "Under the Dome" by Chai Jing.

smith|doorstop Books are a member of Inpress:
www.inpressbooks.co.uk. Distributed by Central Books Ltd.,
99 Wallis Road, London E9 5LN

The Poetry Business is an Arts Council
National Portfolio Organisation

Contents

5	Why that Building is Red
6	Learning to Count: A House by Two Rivers in Winter
7	An Escalator into the Rain
8	The Air
9	Self-Portrait with Facemask
10	Particulate Matter
11	Beijing
12	Three Dragon Day
13	Dongshankou
14	Window Cleaners
15	Year of the Horse
16	Lunch Poem
17	Two Vans
18	Crux
19	无辜
20	混混
21	The Epidemic
22	Self-Portrait with Cicadas and Hornets
23	The Night Bus
25	Talisman
27	Writing Class, Guangzhou
28	Year of the Dragon
29	Heat Lightning
30	A History of the World in Forty Walls

Behind each one walking here hovers a cross that wants to catch up to us, pass us, join us.
Something that wants to sneak up on us from behind and cover our eyes and whisper, "Guess who?"

We look almost happy out in the sun, while we bleed to death from wounds we know nothing about.

– Tomas Tranströmer,
'Streets in Shanghai'

Why that Building is Red

Driving between centres in Shenzhen
my colleague points out the sights:

You see that building? That is where we are going.
It took them just three days to build each floor
which is why we say 'at Shenzhen speed'.

We are driving down the main road in her silver car.
I am flicking through the notes of a class I'll teach later
on brainstorming ideas for a phone app.

And this place here, she gestures, flailing an arm,
This is the best place in town for getting copies.
Shenzhen's most renowned forgerers work here.

We stop at some lights by a large red building.
It looks odd set against the chrome highrises.
Oh and this building, this red one,

this is where people go if they need to be killed.
I look at it more closely. There are two soldiers lounging
at the entrance, a red banner flapping in the breeze.

Of course, that doesn't happen as much any more,
just mainly in the old times. The building is red to warn us
against ghosts. Ghosts are unlucky for business.

The lights change and we leave it behind. It lessens
to the size of a brick, then a smudge. *And here* she says,
slowing the car, *Here is our Starbucks.*

Learning to Count: A House by Two Rivers in Winter

一	a fencepost collapsed under the weight of snow
二	two bodies were floating downstream
三	and the space between them like a third body
四	we doled out our thoughts like spare blankets
五	a man was hobbling down the narrow lane
六	he stopped for breath at our window
七	he rested his arms on the bridge rail
八	the bodies drifted down different rivers
九	the pylons above him were fizzing with giddiness
十	a crucifix was nailed to a whitewashed wall

An Escalator into the Rain

We stand at the bottom of the stairwell
and look up at the storm; raucous lightning
lighting the others. I am among the luckless,
the umbrella-less.

How long have I stood here?
People in bright raincoats take out plastic wallets
and deposit their phones. They board the escalator
like celebrities about to face the paparazzi.

Such storms here, and there's no letting up.
I watch one of the others make a dash for it,
the water is bouncing down the stairs,
the thunder booms. He's gone

and I must go too. I step onto the conveyor
and raise my backpack above my head.
I'm reminded for a moment of boarding a plane,
of knowing there is no going back.

The Air

A text from the embassy: the air today will not be good.
If possible I should stay indoors.
If possible I should wear a mask.
Today is my day off. I sit and watch the air roll in.

The skyscrapers lose their sure angles.
The skyscrapers could almost be whales. I think of Ahab
hurling his pipe. The air buffets against my window.
It is colder inside than outside. The air pants

against the glass. Handprints begin to appear.
Now it's just me. The air mimics the voices of traffic
and hawkers. The traffic and hawkers are drenched in the air.
The walls are starting to sweat.

Self-Portrait with Facemask

I wear it because of the sky,
the sun overhead a filmed eye.

I wear it walking to the metro, respectful
of the wagons' black fumes.

I wear it on the metro, we all do.
We stare at each other like surgeons
during a tricky operation.

I wear it at work. See,
the one correcting grammar on the whiteboard is me.

I start to wear it on dates.
I imagine his slick lips, white rows of teeth.
During sex we leave more than our socks on.

Sometimes I gasp in the night
and raise a hand to my mouth.

I can feel it starting to replace me.
Already my voice is a rasp.

Particulate Matter

This machine will measure your heartbeat
and the lights on the ceiling will display it.

Just hold on to these paddles, please, as though
you were exercising. Breathe deeply.

The air? The air in here is good. Out there?
But we are not out there, are we, sir? Breathe deeply, please.

Look at your measurements. Wear this mask.
At least we are not in Ulaanbaatar. Hold still.

The president has declared a war on the air.
Every possibility is being explored. Deep breaths.

Today is just cloudy, just foggy, dark.
Today there was a windstorm in the Gobi desert.

This is not your concern. Breathe, please. Please stop
asking questions. We are trying to measure your heart.

Beijing

Whenever I'm landing in this city
I'm reminded of the x-rays of my grandfather's chest.

I look down at the roads and remember his ribs,
and passing through the smoggy forcefield

I think about the clouded part above his heart,
and the pain that brought him, proud, to the hospital.

Sometimes in this city of pylons and pagodas
we catch a snatch of blue, fresh air after a typhoon,

and we join the crowds that walk by the river,
all stuffing ourselves full of good air, as if at a buffet.

Three Dragon Day

Forget the science of particulate matter,
air pollution comes from dragons.

On a blue day the dragons are far from the city.
On a day like today the air scratches and growls.

Imagine them, out there, wrapped around skyscrapers,
shrieking to each other through blast furnace throats,

their scales buckled steel, eyes deep as mineshafts,
grey wings rippling with varicose veins.

Putting on a face-mask, a five year old girl
looks out at a city vague as Monet's London.

Today is a three dragon day she says, then heads out
onto the street, towards the crossing, and is gone.

Dongshankou

Sometimes it is enough to come
to the café from the guidebook

and order coffee, an afternoon to marinade
in the pale sunlight, flicking through Szymborska

and copies of the architectural periodicals
that the owner happens to stock.

I am not an architect. I will probably never own a house,
but who is to know in this city, where my tongue

can't negotiate even simple consonants,
where the coffee I've ordered arrives as tea,

where the door opposite me suddenly widens a crack
and a stranger takes my picture.

Window Cleaners

They stand on the tops of skyscrapers
like toy soldiers, they of the pole-system,
the lowering box.

Today they are abseiling down Huaxia Plaza,
one hundred floors of prime location
and not a unit of it let.

I imagine them as deep sea gravediggers,
as tiny fish that nibble the flesh between toes,
blind masseurs tasked with a sperm whale,

or just as they are: men on thin winches,
pummelling their feet against the bomb proof glass,
washing away footprints as they drop.

Next to them another building is going up,
cranes lifting girders, planks of wood.
As night falls we see sparks fall from high floors

and the window cleaners pause a moment, look up
at the new biggest building, a hundred and ten floors
of prime location and, so far, none of it let.

Year of the Horse

All week the students have been masking dalahästs,
folding red card into flanks and manes,
gold-penning hooves and eyes.

In reception they've made a giant one
and stapled it a harness of money.
A horse means lucky, and money on a horse

means extra lucky, the students say, thickening
the saddle. I think back on my own luck and remember
those three horses in a Pennine paddock.

They would come to the edge of the dry stone wall
and you would feed them vegetables, long grass,
although they had a field of it, and knew the story of grass.

They'd lift it from your hand, offering you
their shy necks, and you'd say that life as a horse
would be better than this one, saddled with debts,

each of us burdened with invisible riders.

Lunch Poem

The construction workers have lunch at noon.
They unplug their circular saws, put down their sledgehammers
and head to the nearby park.

It is then that the Guangzhou Treetop Orchestra of Cicadas
launches into its great insecty opus:
GET UP!   BUILD!   CREATE!

Two Vans

Ayi is going for her ultrasound
in the white van on the outskirts.

She's been throwing up in the closet
each morning for a week.

It's that bug that's going around
is what she tells the boss.

If it's a boy she will hand in her notice.
If it's a girl she will schedule another appointment

with the man who drives the black van.
Last time she stuck the photo to the ceiling

and stared and stared at it, until her eyes blurred,
and it dissolved, and was gone.

Crux

There are no constellations in this city.
The closest thing we have is the night traffic
I watch thicken on the super expressway
from the hundredth floor of the IFC.

It's 6pm. The lights rebound off other lights.
The rush hour congestion reflects the flight path
and the moon peers in through the smog
like a man who has stopped by a window.

There are people here who have never known
the intimacy of stars. I look out over the city
and think of that advert surrounding the slum.

A boy is playing a violin for his grandparents.
They wear smiles and seem to be clapping.
Someone has cut out his eyes.

无辜

A message on we-chat. One of the villagers
has lost it. He's climbed to the top of the old pagoda
and unfurled a banner: innocent.

A crowd has gathered, munching cucumbers.
They speculate how he made it through the thick
barbed wire. The police arrive, plug in a loudspeaker

and try to coax him down. *What is he innocent of?*
we ask, *Uncle*, the police shout, *Uncle come down*.
The villager grips on to his banner. The sun slinks

behind the pagoda. People begin to leave.
The police keep asking to look at my passport.
They keep checking my phone for a camera.

The villager stayed up there for almost three days.
As the sun set he suddenly lifted his head
and screamed, *Innocent! Innocent! I'm innocent!*

then jumped.

The police stood around a while after he'd hit.
They made quiet notes and shook their heads.
They carried him off. They folded up the banner.

混混

The migrant worker has a grievance.
He is writing it down on the flagstones
of Tiyu Xilu, ideograph by ideograph

using different sticks of coloured chalk
and a single slab for each character.
I can't read much but I know good writing.

I recognise *no* and *trouble* and *person* and *can't*.
The other passers-by pause a little
then move on, glancing over their shoulders,

shepherding away their children.
Someone taps him lightly on the back.
They are coming your way, they whisper.

The migrant worker shakes his head and laughs.
He looks left and right for their light blue tunics.
They are approaching him from every direction.

The Epidemic

We are watching a film about the epidemic
when he asks what the black spots are
and why they appear and won't wash off
and why this doesn't ever happen in China.

I switch on the VPN and google *China, lesion images*
then watch his eyes, swivelling between bath houses,
some recent footage from a clinic in Chengdu
and the cut-off AIDS villages of Henan province.

He turns off the VPN and searches *China, lesion images*
then shows me the first video. A doctor is staring deep
into the camera, *this disease is spread by foreigners
and homosexuals. Since opening the borders infection rates*

have rocketed. I only understand him after translation.
I listen again, to this man's lilting Beijing accent.
I stare into his reasonable, almost-kind eyes,
then jab the screen, which loads the next video.

Self-Portrait with Cicadas and Hornets

It is sometimes enough to wake late, make coffee
and sit on the stern wooden bench we use as a sofa
where you use me, in turn, as a headrest, and I run
the fingers of my left hand along your buzzcut
and rest my right wrist on your heart, unsure
if the pulse I feel comes from my wrist or your heart
or a mix of the two, just as all summer the cicadas
and construction workers have battled to tear up the air.

I step out to the balcony and stare down at the market.
It's citrus season again, and villagers are unloading
a minibus of pomelos, mangosteens and small caged rabbits,
the kind with quick breath and cloudy eyes, that lie still.
And there sits the man selling six nests of hornets,
no-one goes near him, but every day he's there,
his hornets reverberating against the sides of their nets
as he sits with his head in his hands.

The Night Bus

I wake in the night to find we're driving past
the famous UNESCO site, stone Buddhas glowing

among the ruined stupas, dogs eyes igniting
by the roadside. Only me and the driver awake

and nothing seems changed – the pagoda drifts past
on its rise as we take the long bend past my old school.

It must be ten years. We approach Don Po roundabout,
cruise past the all-night noodle stalls and I see the stages

being erected for the egg banana festival –
a week of dancing for a fruit! – and then up,

up over the river. I can hear crickets chatter
through the undergrowth and think of him, still here

on the far side of town, with a wife now, a child.
The last time I came he told her we were going to play snooker

and she looked at me knowing we wouldn't play snooker.
It must be ten years. The river under me shifts like a sinister figure.

I see the other bridge flicker at the far side of town, the moths
still clattering into every streetlamp and then we're over, slowing,

the driver announcing the stop. You stir from your dream and ask if I know
where we are. *The middle of nowhere*, I say, and your eyes slowly close.

Kamphaeng Phet? calls the driver, *Kamphaeng Phet?*
And the door shuts out the singing air.

Talisman

I don't need an amulet
around my neck, don't need a jade bracelet

upon my wrist, a twist of string, blessed
around my shin. I don't need onions

or jasmine above my door, don't need to live
on the eighth floor of this apartment complex,

could take the fourth bed on any ward
and not fear death. And I don't need the Lord

Buddha on my dashboard, nor a bible on the table
beside our bed, and I won't throw blind dice

at 3a.m. to test chance as if chance were a test.
And I don't need a lucky cat to lure you back

as if my life were a shop and my heart on sale,
as if the others who had rummaged through

the discount rails hadn't left
dry-washing their hands.

But what I need are your lectures on mess
and you laughing as I panic on flights

and your breath in the small hours
steadying the room, as the passengers above us

begin their descents, the captain requesting
the cabin crew be seated, releasing the aeroplane's wheels.

Writing Class, Guangzhou

I ask them to bring in a thing
that they care for. They bring:

a hairpin carved in the shape
of a carp; a policeman's flask;

young elephants engulfed
by their mother's trunk, a statue;

a picture of a rabbit, the only toy
they left her after joining school.

One lady has brought in her husband.
He sits in the corner sipping lemon tea.

The others: a silver coin that dates
from the Qing dynasty; a string of pearls

that survived The Great Leap Forward;
the only surviving photo of a family.

She remembers the day it was taken,
her sister crying and not keeping still,

the hesitation she felt looking into the lens,
her father's hands gripping her shoulders.

Year of the Dragon

I remember sitting around the woodburner
in Deirdre's back garden, the lighthouse beam

flitting from sea to land to sea, and Ian
reciting the poem by MacNeice from memory:

We are dying, Egypt, dying, at a time when
Egypt really was, the squares full of protests

and later full of bodies, and all the politicians
taking turns to condemn and praise and condemn,

as if they too were lighthouses, spinning out
their light in the dark. Then Mary joined in,

and I remember thinking what a thing it was
to hear two people remembering, to hear Ireland

and Yorkshire in the same breath, the same hymn,
to hear voices strengthen for the same loved parts

and then diminish, so that all that was left
was kindling, blistering in the dark.

Heat Lightning

We get woken in the small hours
by the flashing sky, rush from our tent

and start to peg down the tarp
that does for our shelter. I look up

at the sulphurous night, the few far stars
and the flashes that say:

*thunder is coming and all manner
of weather.* The waves graze the sand

as silent lightning ignites, as if the stars
were taking our photograph. The waves clatter

the shore, but still I feel we'll be okay,
that tomorrow's sea will juggle our boat to the harbour

and you'll mutter again in your seasick voice
that English men all smell of rain.

A History of the World in Forty Walls

A biting Autumn day.
The cable car lifts me up from grey Beijing
and drops me here,
with sky we haven't had in months,
with three hours to walk where I want.
I undo my facemask and take it in.

It was built as a defense against northern barbarians
and stretches for over six thousand kilometers.
It's the only wall in the world that really matters ...

But what about the other walls?
The West wall of Jerusalem,
the Walls of Constantinople, Dubrovnik,
the West Bank Barrier?
What about fallen walls: Berlin, Jericho, Hadrian's,
the wall in Belfast they called the Peace Line,
the crumbling Wall of Western Sahara?

And then there's Phnom Penh, York, Ayuthaya.

Or those joking walls: the sticky gum wall of Seattle
And Kamphaeng Phet (the diamond wall) with its
looted Buddhas.

We climb The Great Wall
with our manic cameras
and I'm thinking of something humbler:
the wall my mother pressed a glass against

in our rough end terrace,
the wall we played football against,
the wall by the river
and its hidden footholds
and the day it let me fall.

Childhood walls: the truants' wall,
the redbrick walls of Woodhouse Ridge
the pebbledashed paper-round estate walls,
dry stone walls, the ruined dam near Helvellyn
we called Jean-Claude.

The snowline,
which was a kind of wall,
the cairn that marked out
Swirrel Edge, the little shelters
that dotted high fells,
the crying walls of Guangzhou in the spring
and the walls of the knackered slum
covered in slogans
and the people still living there regardless, holding out
for a better deal
as new walls rose around them.

Super expressways,
which are another wall.

High speed rail links, the people who had to
up and leave,
the cataract of smog from here to Hong Kong.
Ramparts,

barricades,
markers,
territories,
border crossings,
trade zones.
Good walls make good neighbours.

Why don't they go back to where they came from?

A house with love has elastic walls.

*If you press a spring too hard
it will snap back. You must always remember this.*

And this:
*We grope along the wall like blind men,
We grope like those who have no eyes;
We stumble at midday as in the twilight,
Among those who are vigorous we are like dead men.*